St Ives

I remember looking at St Ives – from the height (
further up from Tregena Steps – it was the perfe

Norman ....., ...

T he quaint old fishing port of St Ives is situated on the north coast of Cornwall to the west of the Hayle estuary, in an areawhose fates and fortunes have long been governed by the movement of sand and tides.

Archaeological discoveries in the immediate vicinity of St Ives, including several Neolithic stone axes, would indicate that the site has been inhabited since ancient times. An early settlement is thought to have been established around the fortified headland of Pendinas, and across the isthmus, where traces of walls and other ruins have been found beneath the sands. The little fishing village of long ago, which became known as Porthia, probably fringed the shores from the Castle Rocks to the foot of Skidden Hill. It grew in importance as the anciently established port of Lelant became overwhelmed by accumulations of sand swept in from the sea, and St Ives itself was obliged to retreat to higher levels on account of the continuing build up of sand. By the mid nineteenth century the prosperous port, market and corporate town was expanding up the steep hillside into its mineral-rich hinterland.

This house in Fish Street is reputedly the oldest in St Ives.

St Ia

The tiny fishing settlement, anciently known as Pendennis, Pendinas or Pendunes, indicating a fortified headland, became known as Porthia (the port of Ia) after the arrival of an Irish saint of that name around 450 AD. The name of the expanding port, which came to be known as Sancta Ye, Saynt Iyes and Saint Ithes over the centuries, eventually emerged as Saint Ives.

According to ancient tradition, this fervently Christian daughter of an Irish chieftain, had set her heart on joining Prince Fingar (Gwinear) and his many followers on a missionary expedition to alien shores. When he refused to take her, she put to sea in a tiny coracle, trusting that God would guide her in her quest to convert the heathen and save souls. The inhabitants of the place which was destined to bear her name were astonished to see the maiden come ashore in what they took to be an outsized leaf with its sides turned up, for Irish coracles were unfamiliar around these parts. It is thought that she came ashore at Porthminster, which became the

St Ives harbour with Smeaton's Pier on the right.

site of an oratory which would later be destroyed by French marauders).

Although the main band of missionaries had set their sights on Brittany, prevailing winds and currents eventually carried the large flotilla into St Ives Bay, much to the consternation of the local population. On landing it soon became apparent that their gentle, spurned disciple was well established, with a faithful band of followers. As the zealous arrivals swarmed on across the Hayle estuary and over Connor Downs, intent on preaching the good news and saving sinners, they were set upon by the local King Teudar, and scattered in all directions. Some said that their leader Fingar, who sustained a serious neck injury, retreated to Gwinear with his head tucked underneath his arm. Other followers also suffered, lending their names to Uny Lelant and Phillack. St Ia's bones were venerated in the ancient oratory for centuries, and later transferred to the parish church. They disappeared at the time of the Reformation.

Pendinas

St Nicholas chapel.

Old St Ives had quaint and narrow streets, many of which remain.

Porthminster

Tradition tells us that the commanding headland of Pendinas, later known as The Island or St Ives Head, was formerly a tidal island which became linked to the mainland as the result of an extraordinary influx of sand. This was thought to explain the irregularity of streets in the older part of the town, adjoining the Island. Traces of an ancient stronghold remain on the summit of the headland, where the original chapel of St Nicholas stood, before the church was constructed. This ancient fishermen's chapel had a chequered history, having been used as a look-out for Customs men, a refuge for pilots and wartime store, before being demolished by the War Office in 1904. It was rebuilt in 1911 by Sir Edward Hain (of ship-owning fame), and further restored in 1971. A battery of heavy guns was emplaced in this strategic position on an embattled platform, known as the Castle. This was manned by a sergeant of the coast-guard and one gunner. It was dismantled in 1895, when some of the material was used in the construction of a former jetty.

In the mid sixteenth century a pharos (or beacon) stood on the headland for the guidance of shipping. The adjacent cove of Porthgwidden, then described as 'an indifferent safe road for ships to lie at anchor with some winds', opened up opportunities for mercantile trade as well as the fishing industry. The Island was traditionally used for the drying of fishing nets, which were steeped in an oak bark preservative after every use. These out-spread nets made the Island appear black from a distance, but generations of grazing cattle were conditioned to cope with this unusual situation.

Porthminster, to the east of the harbour, was once the site of an oratory and fishing village. High above Porthminster Point was a house where huers kept watch for signs of approaching pilchard shoals, and directed the activities of the seine boats.

By the end of the fourteenth century St Ives was a thriving little fishing town with its mother church three miles away, at the once important port of Lelant, then declining on account of the silting up of the harbour. In 1408 the townsfolk petitioned for a church of their own, and the handsome church of St Ia with its battlemented tower came to be built between 1410 and 1434 as a chapel-of-ease. It was said to have been constructed of granite brought round by sea from Zennor. According to tradition there was formerly a field between this salt-sprayed church and the sea, where sheep were put to graze. But it was swept away by a terrific hurricane which overwhelmed part of the town with sand and seawater, probably in the seventeenth century.

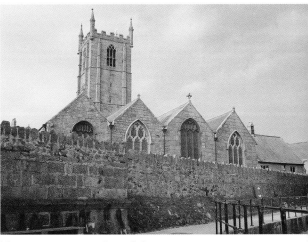

Church of St Ia.

The delightful little chapel of St Leonards, which still stands on the old quay, is a reminder of the time when prayers were said for the fishermen before they put to sea. They donated a portion of their catch to the friar for his services. The fishermen and miners of St Ives gave John and Charles Wesley a very rough ride when they first appeared on the scene. However, the Wesleys eventually overcame the suspicion and hostility, and made a lasting impact on the place. They preached in people's houses, barns, sheds and shelters, or in the open air. The market place provided a convenient focal point, capable of accommodating a large crowd. A profusion of chapels and meeting houses was subsequently established throughout the area, catering for Wesleyans and a host of splinter groups and independent sects. The Salvation Army Citadel on the Wharf next to the old RNLI Boathouse, established in 1879, offered practical help when disaster struck, as it frequently did in this hardy seafaring community. A Catholic church was built in 1908.

Events of National Importance

Perkin Warbeck

The market house built in 1832, occupies the site of an earlier one, which owed its existence to Sir Robert Willoughby, whose influence had obtained the privilege of a weekly Saturday market and two annual fairs.

Although Cornwall might have been regarded as far removed from mainstream Britain, St Ives had connections with events and people of national importance. In August 1496 Perkin Warbeck, pretender to the throne and his wife the Lady Catherine Gordon, arrived here from Ireland with four ships of war and about 150 men. This person asserted that he was the Duke of York, who was generally believed to have been murdered in the Tower with his brother the King, by the order of Richard III. He was proclaimed Richard IV in the town. Then he and his followers proceeded to St Michael's Mount, where the lady was placed in the castle, while the troops marched on towards Bodmin.

The imposition of the English Prayer Book struck a bitter chord with the Cornish in 1549, who sought to restore their Catholic religion with the services and rituals they had always known. This led to an uprising in which John Payne, the portrieve of St Ives became one of the captains in a rebel army led by Sir Humphrey Arundell. After being decisively beaten at Exeter, the survivors dispersed and made their ragged way home. Shortly afterwards, Sir Anthony Kingston, the Provost Marshall, was dispatched westwards to seek out and punish the traitors. The king's representative hanged the Mayor of Bodmin, and when he arrived in St Ives the troubled portrieve pre-

pared a sumptuous entertainment for him, hoping that his part in the affair had been forgotten.

Everyone was enjoying the prestigious occasion, and the wine was flowing freely when the portrieve fancied that he heard a hammering noise just outside in the market place. A ghastly suspicion crossed his befuddled mind, but was dispelled when Sir Anthony informed him with great geniality that they were merely about to hang a wretched rebel. When they had gorged enough, the commissioner took hold of his host's arm in courtly style, and led him outside to inspect the gallows. 'What say you, Master Portrieve?' he asked most courteously. 'Is yon gibbet duly furnished for the hanging of a traitor?' 'All seems ready, if't please you, Sir,' he replied with due deference. 'Then,' commanded the royal commissioner, summoning a man-at-arms, 'Secure Master Payne, who hath been a busy rebel, and hang him forthwith. For such is the King's pleasure!' There were loud protestations and a brief struggle before the leading citizen of St Ives was strung up and speedily dispatched.

In 1644 the men of St Ives, Towednack and Zennor assembled on Longstone Downs in support of the Parliamentarians, and when Sir Richard Grenville marched into the west with a strong body of Royalists to check their proceedings, he discovered about 200 rebels armed with swords and muskets and other weapons.

The introduction of the English Prayer Book causes an uprising

The Civil War

The branch line at Carbis Bay, near to the place where the Parliamentarian sympathisers gathered.

When the local army realised that they were outnumbered, they decided that discretion was the better part of valour, took to their heels and scattered in all directions. The King's troops later entered the town, and the unlucky Mayor was held responsible for not subduing their rebellious spirit. His failure to pay the £500 fine levied by Sir Richard resulted in his being committed to Launceston Goal. Before leaving the town Sir Richard ordered a Zennor man to be hanged, and the following day a St Ives man was hanged at Helston and another man was put to death in Truro. Captain Arundell, who headed the rebels, was proclaimed a traitor and ordered to be hanged when captured. But he escaped and went on to serve the Parliamentarians under General Fairfax. When a Royalist army under Colonel Goring subsequently attempted to march on the town, the men of St Ives were able to keep them at bay by blocking the roads with heavy pilchard caskets weighted with sand, and maintaining such a strong guard that they were obliged to divert to Penzance.

Plague

Although the folk of St Ives had suffered casualties on account of being caught up in politics, the greatest threat to the population was pestilence, often brought into the port by rat-infested ships. In 1647 a terrible plague broke out, carrying off over 500 people. Many fled, and the market was closed down for some considerable time. Some supplies were brought to the banks of streams bordering the parish, where the money left could be cleansed by the water. More people would have perished from famine than the plague, had not a vessel from Plymouth, laden with corn and wine, sought shelter in the harbour. Its cargo was purchased by the Mayor and other gentlemen, and distributed to the distressed.

Godrevy Island.

The Civil War ended with victory for the Parliamentarians, and on 30 July 1648, the day on which Charles I was executed, the Topsham vessel *Garland* carrying his wardrobe and possessions and that of his fugitive queen, was dashed to pieces on the rocks of

Godrevy Island during a terrible thunderstorm. Of the sixty or so aboard, all were lost apart from a man, a boy and a dog, who swam ashore and survived on seaweed and rainwater for two days before being rescued. Some say that the queen's jewels were discovered by a humble cottager on Gwithian beach a few days later. There was jubilation in St Ives in 1653 when Oliver Cromwell was proclaimed as Lord Protector of the realm, and about 100 militia men wearing blue and white ribbons round their hats, fired three volleys and distributed hogsheads of beer. Major Ceely was appointed vice admiral of the district by Cromwell at that time, with a troop of horse under his command.

The Queen's jewels beached in Gwithian

In 1685 the vessel *Rising Sun* brought the Duke of Monmouth here from Holland. He and his followers eventually landed at Lyme Regis, entering into the desperate Western Rebellion, which ended in disaster on the field of Sedgemoor.

The Monmouth Rebellion

The port of St Ives had always been vulnerable to seaborne attack, particularly in times of war, and in 1776, when the American War of Independence broke out, their defences were strengthened by the delivery of a quantity of guns and ammunition by the sloop *Endeavour*. During the Napoleonic wars their defences were further strengthened, while a number of Sea Fencibles patrolled the coastal waters. The Revenue Cruiser *Dolphin*, whose principal task was to stifle the activities of the Free Traders, also protected shipping, escorted convoys and served as a lifeboat and salvage vessel.

A slick Revenue cutter in pursuit of a smuggling vessel.

Borough of St Ives

St Ives became a borough in 1558, when it was governed by a portrieve and burgesses. The Portrieve commanded great authority, overseeing the harbour, the fisheries, the church and all the affairs of the town, including disputes. The first charter, incorporated by Charles I in 1639, was forfeited in 1685, then renewed by James II in 1686. The borough returned two members of Parliament from 1558 until the Reform Act of 1832. Sir Frances Bassett, who was instrumental in obtaining the first charter, presented a silver cup to the corporation, bearing the quaint inscription:

If any discord should arise,
Within the borough of St Ives,
'Tis my desire this Cup of Love,
An instrument of Peace may prove.

This charming scene showing the Mary Ann II on the left and a 6-oared gig on the right makes it difficult to imagine the bloody skirmishes that have taken place in St Ives Bay.

Swashbuckling Exploits

This coast was much infested with Turkish pirates during the seventeenth century, and was the scene of many a seafaring skirmish. On one occasion the fishermen of St Ives brought in two Irish vessels laden with rum and staves, whose crews had supposedly been carried off at sea. Sir John Arundell, who took possession of them when they reached the port allowed the finders to keep one of the prize ships, and sent the other one up to Padstow. A particularly colourful exploit of 1635 involved a Turkish pirate ship of 12 guns, which attacked three small vessels from Fowey and Looe, captured the crew and held them on deck, before setting their vessels adrift. Some time later, while the pirate ship was cruising in the Channel, the English sailors hatched a plot, whereby at a given signal, the captain would be felled with the capstan bar and tossed overboard. The element of surprise allowed them to turn the tables on their Turkish captors, who were held below deck while the English sailors took control of the ship, and headed for St Ives. The angry Turks were firing shots up through the deck as favourable winds brought them in to port, where they were retained by the authorities before being sent back to their own country.

Turkish pirates

Rum smuggling

French barques

In 1654, Thomas Purefoy, captain of a small privateer belonging to Major Ceely, captured five French barques laden with salt, and brought them into St Ives. A number of other French prizes were brought into the harbour over the next few years, while valuable cargoes from vessels wrecked around the coast were similarly taken

Dutch ships

to the vice admiral's house at St Ives. In 1705 a Dutch ship and a packet ship bound for Lisbon were chased into St Ives by a French privateer. Her response to being fired at by the Castle guns was to let fly with her guns in the direction of the town before beating a hasty retreat.

There was great consternation in December 1781, when a large

French cutter

French cutter entered St Ives Bay, and lay at anchor just off shore. She leapt into action on Christmas Day, when the lugger *Phoenix* came in sight, and a violent skirmish ensued, during which Captain Davey and the crew of the smaller vessel demonstrated great skill and courage. After taking a terrible battering, the lugger went down stern first, but fortunately an English cutter appeared on the scene, and was able to rescue the captain and 22 of the crew.

French slave trader

In February 1826 Lieut. G.H. Rye and his sailors of the Coastguard took possession of a 20 gun French slave trader, fitted with boarding spikes and bristling with firearms and other weaponry, which had been forced into St Ives by stormy weather. This was her fourteenth slave voyage in eight years, despite the fact that Napoleon had ended the slave trade in 1815. The kind-hearted officer released a trembling negro child from his cruel master's grip, and took him home to his own five motherless children.

One night in November 1815, the officers of the Preventive boat in the service of the Customs who had seized between 200 and 300 casks of smuggled spirits on the shore, were violently attacked by a large band of smugglers who succeeded in carrying off the contraband. The Custom House in London offered a reward of £200 for information leading to their conviction.

Smuggling

St Ives was well suited for piratical and smuggling exploits, situated as it was on the old trading route to the prosperous port of Bristol, which had links with Ireland, the Mediterranean and the West Indies. Vessels carrying valuable cargoes such as wines, tea, tobacco, rum and sugar, could be intercepted by coastal traders, and the contraband transferred to smaller boats and landed on these expansive beaches.

The wars with France affected the fish trade, and the heavy duties that Pitt levied on salt, essential for curing pilchards, led to smuggled salt. Sometimes large catches of pilchards were left in nets submerged in shallow water, until an illicit cargo of salt became available.

The profusion of caves, mine adits and underground tunnels along this section of coast were ideal places to conceal illicit goods, before being spirited away elsewhere. Smuggling was a way of life here, with some of the activity centred on the harbour, under the noses of the authorities. Indeed, certain eminent townsfolk, including the Mayor John Knill, were thought to have been involved, and rumour had it that Bristol merchants came to St Ives to purchase uncustomed sugar. Kegs of brandy were stored in the church at Lelant in the early nineteenth century.

The trading schooner Glenfeadon outside the harbour.

Much of the subversive planning was carried out in the taverns of St Ives, and much of the swag and swagger was centred on 'Hicks's Court'. In the mid-nineteenth century two colourful characters known as 'Old Tubs' and 'Old Worms' held the other customers spellbound in the *Sloop Inn*, with their tales of derring-do. It was said that the sight of the red coat and cocked hat of an Exciseman were like a red rag to an infuriated bull as far as these old timers were concerned.

Map of St Ives showing places named in the text

The dominating headland, known as The Island, is linked to the mainland by an isthmus. An anchorage with protective piers was created on the eastern side of the isthmus at Porth Cocking, between Bamaluz Point and Pedn Olva, where large numbers of seine boats were traditionally drawn up. The now residential area of Carbis Bay was formerly the scene of intense industrial activity, forming part of a network of tin and copper mines in the wild and hilly hinterland of St Ives, with its lonely moors and granite tors. The conspicuous white lighthouse on the little island of Godrevy across St Ives Bay, is a salutory reminder that this recreational area was once awesome shipwreck territory.

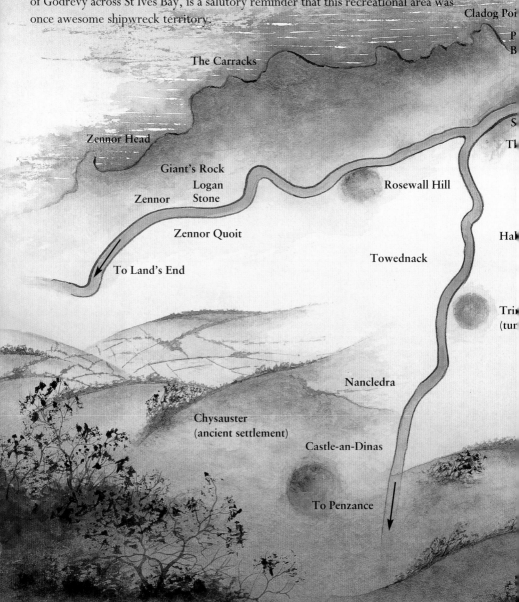

Cladog Poi

P

B

The Carracks

Zennor Head

S

Tl

Giant's Rock

Logan
Stone

Rosewall Hill

Zennor

Zennor Quoit

Ha

Towednack

To Land's End

Tri
(tur

Nancledra

Chysauster
(ancient settlement)

Castle-an-Dinas

To Penzance

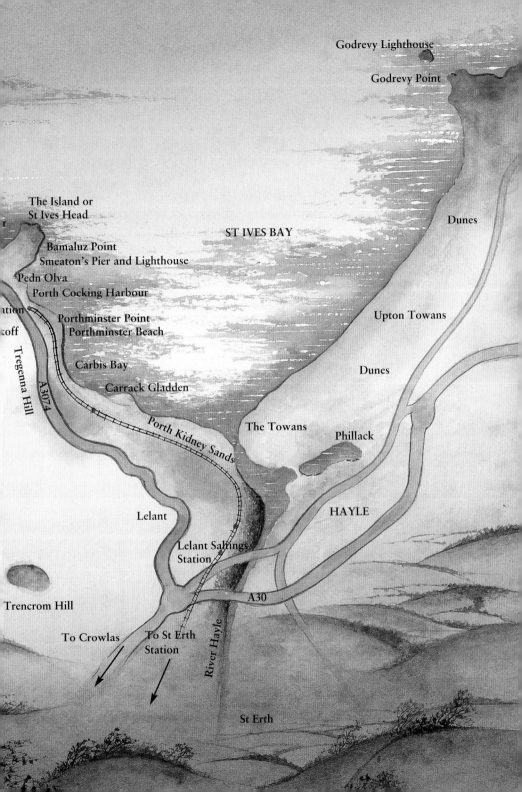

Godrevy Lighthouse

Godrevy Point

The Island or
St Ives Head

Dunes

ST IVES BAY

Bamaluz Point
Smeaton's Pier and Lighthouse

Pedn Olva
Porth Cocking Harbour

Upton Towans

ation

koff

Porthminster Point
Porthminster Beach

Dunes

Carbis Bay

Carrack Gladden

The Towans

Phillack

Porth Kidney Sands

HAYLE

Lelant

Lelant Saltings
Station

Trencrom Hill

A30

To Crowlas

To St Erth
Station

River Hayle

St Erth

The Need to Create a Safe Haven

Traditionally, fishing boats and small trading vessels were drawn up on the shores of creeks along this rather inhospitable north coast, where the local population fished in fair weather. But there were on-going attempts to create a safe anchorage here in the days of sail, for the protection of shipping and to exploit the potential of maritime trade and industry. In the late seventeenth century the Coasting Pylot described the situation of St Ives as being, 'Four Leagues to the Eastward of Cape Cornwall, in a Sandy Bay', where 'Vessels lie aground at Low water'. *Murray's Handbook of Devon & Cornwall* fills in more of the story in the middle of the nineteenth century: 'The pier was constructed in 1767 by Smeaton, the architect of the Eddystone lighthouse, and a breakwater was commenced in 1816, but abandoned after an outlay of £5,000. It would have rendered the bay a secure anchorage, which is now exposed to the north and east. The project, however, may yet be carried out, s the completion of the breakwater was recommended by a committee of the House of Commons in 1859, and the fitness of St Ives for a harbour of refuge is under consideration.' History shows that a proposed New Pier on the seaward side of Smeaton's Pier, started in 1864, was unable to withstand batterings from the sea, the Victoria Extension to Smeaton's Pier was completed in 1890, with its octagonal iron lighthouse becoming operational that September, and the West Pier was completed in 1894. Vessels still lie aground at low water.

Remains of old wooden pier.

Maritime Activity

One of the most formidable seafaring hazards in the days of sail, was the partly submerged reef of rocks on the north-eastern tip of St Ives Bay, which gave rise to a seemingly endless catalogue of disasters over the centuries. But it was the dramatic wrecking of the fast and splendid iron, screw passenger steamer *Nile* in 1854, in which everyone lost their lives, that led to the building of a lighthouse on Godrevy Island to warn mariners of the dangers. The lighthouse first cast its rays across these waters in 1859.

St Ives became the purposeful scene of multifarious maritime activity, with master mariners, pilots, sailors, coastguards, custom men and fishermen thronging the quayside, where shipwrights, anchor smiths, sail-makers, rope and net-makers plied their trade.

Time was, when the celebrated pilots of St Ives, or 'hobblers' as they were known around these parts, made a profitable living from pilotage and salvage work; time was when the harbour was a sea of masts, and the fishing so abundant, and the smell of fish so intense that the vicar feared it would stop the church clock. Those were the days when rescues were carried out by ever watchful local seafarers, using a variety of craft, including small naval ship's boats and cork-lined boats.

Pilots, with their specialised knowledge of the vagaries of local waters were renowned for their skill and daring, and played a vital role in the preservation of life from shipwreck. (Sheila Bird Collection)

The Hain family, who were ship owners in the days of sail, operated one of the world's oldest and most renowned tramp steamer fleets, with a company office in the town. *The Hain Steamship Company* was established in 1901 by Sir Edward Hain, and the enterprise brought wealth and recognition to St Ives. The tragic loss of his son in World War I and his own death in 1917, led to the company being taken over by P & O later that year, and the office being transferred to London.

Unloading goods from a trading vessel alongside Smeaton's Pier in 1905.

Preserving Life from Shipwreck

Tucking the Seine nets.

Many disastrous shipwrecks occurred along this awesome section of coast, where daring rescues were spontaneously carried out by the local seafaring fraternity. During the nineteenth century fishermen, pilots, coastguards and others received official recognition for their bravery in the form of medals or monetary awards on various occasions. There had been many attempts to raise enough money to provide a lifeboat since the beginning of the nineteenth century, and it was quite a breakthrough when a St Ives shipbuilder won a competition to design a lifeboat, and the 30-foot *Hope* was emplaced here. There was great excitement in 1861 when the RNLI established a station at St Ives, and crowds were enthralled to witness the highly professional crew in lifejackets performing spectacular capers with their self-righting lifeboat *Moses*.

The distinguished service record as displayed in the modern Boathouse demonstrates the exceptional skill and bravery of on-going generations of lifeboatmen. The terrible tragedies of January 1938 and January 1939, in which the Coxwain and crew members lost their lives will never be forgotten. In more recent years the pattern has tended towards an increasing number of services to holidaymakers and pleasure craft, interspersed with fishermen in distress and some major catastrophes, like that of the *Secil Japan* in ferocious seas, reminding us that although technology may become more sophisticated, the sea does not mellow with age.

Packing pilchards into casks at a cellar around 1890.

Fishing

The fishermen of St Ives have long been famous for their expertise in catching fish, and for centuries the industry was the enduring source of local revenue and pride. At one time a wide variety of species frequented these waters, and pilchards and herrings were in great abundance. The most ancient method of fishing was called drifting, where boats out at sea trailed nets which trapped the fish by the gills. Seine fishing, where the boats worked together with weighted nets strung out between them was effective in trapping shoals. Huers on the cliffs directed operations, initially with semaphore type signals and later megaphones, enabling fish to become encircled then scooper up with the aid of 'tucking' nets.

When the boats returned the fish would be brought ashore in smaller boats or loaded into horse-drawn carts on the beach, according to the state of the tide. Women worked in the fish market on the quayside, where fish would be smoked or salted and pressed before being exported to Spain or Italy.

There was great excitement during the nineteenth century, when epic catches were proudly borne into port. Children rushed around shouting 'Heva! Heva!', while the town crier strutted through the streets in his high pole hat giving details of the pay-outs in the taverns. In the early part of that century fish caught around these shores were taken to Bristol, where they were purchased by dealers, and conveyed to Billingsgate in vans or light carts. Mackerel was supplied to the home market, and some fishwives were known to have travelled over 20 miles a day, carrying more than one hundredweight of fish on their heads to neighbouring parishes. Every cottage Down'long had its own cellar for barking nets and storing sails, crabpots and other work-a-day equipment.

Mining

In the late eighteenth century, an overland traveller described St Ives as being 'in the midst of mines, and open to a very fine bay'. In fact there was a profusion of tin and copper mines throughout the parish, and tin streaming, which is the most rudimentary form of mining had been carried out for centuries. Tin was once streamed in the waters of the *Stennack*, which runs steeply down the centre of the town, and is piped through a tunnel with the outfall just behind the RNLI Boathouse. In olden times the surface miners dug, shovelled and sifted the material washed down from the high moors, extracting grains of black tin for the silt and sand. As the technology became available, a number of deep underground workings were established, including *Trenwith*, above the *Stennack*, *Pednolver*, *Wheal Margery* (on Porthminster Point, which ran out under the sea), *Wheal Snuff* (on The Island above Porthmeor Beach), *Wheal Dream* (where the Museum is now sited) and *Wheal Providence* at Carbis Bay. The tin streamers and miners lived *Up 'long* in the *Stennack*, while the fisherfolk dwelt *Down 'long*. Each community had a distinctive culture.

The first copper ores to be shipped from St Ives were said to have been from *Wheal Trenwith*, aboard the *Pulmanter* and *Betsy*, in May 1826. Ores were also shipped to St Ives and thence to Neath for smelting from the copper mine at St Just, for fuel was scarce in north Cornwall. The vessels returned with coal and Welsh timber for the mines. Centuries ago several copper lodes were worked at Lelant, and generations of vicars enjoyed the royalties from mines on the glebelands, until the sands blew in and overwhelmed the area.

Mine owner James Halse constructed the village of Halsetown, providing about a hundred dwellings, a school and several chapels to accommodate the miners. This occupancy of housing gave the miners the franchise, thus helping to return their benefactor as MP for St Ives.

Sir Henry Irving, the noted classical actor, spent part of his childhood in Halsetown.

The celebrated Wheal Providence *at Carbis Bay, which exploited tin and copper employed hundreds of people in the nineteenth century, and had galleries running far out under the sea.*

Life and Customs in Old St Ives

Strangers to the old sea port were captivated by the picturesque, work-a-day charm of the waterfront, where proud weather-beaten faces, sou' westers, oilskins, guernseys and long sea boots were much in evidence. Life revolved around the harbour, the chapel and the church, which served the spiritual and social needs of the whole family throughout the year, with special celebrations on high days and holidays. There was great excitement as travelling shows and fairs came to town, pitching their tents on the Island. The *St Ives Pig Fair* or *Fair-Mo*, recalls the days when cottagers brought their pigs to market to raise a little money just before Christmas, and sweet and confectionary stalls were set up in the main street. Hurling the silver ball on Feast Monday, guise dancing and the quinquennial Knill ceremony were also time-honoured customs peculiar to St Ives.

When eighteenth century Mayor, Customs official (and unofficial smuggler) John Knill built the pyramidal, granite steeple on the top of Worvas Hill, he intended it to be his own mausoleum. In his will he directed that there should be a five yearly ceremony whereby ten little maidens dressed in white, accompanied by two widows, a clergyman, fiddler, Custom Officer and the Mayor of

St Ives, should come here on St James' Day to sing the Old Hundredth Psalm, and dance and sing for fifteen minutes to the music of the fiddler. As it happened, he died elsewhere, and the sarcophagus remained empty.

Alfred Wallis, who became famous as a painter, was well acquainted with this area of St Ives.

Left *Fetching water in Down 'long in 1906.*

The Knill festivities of 1896.

The Arrival of the Railway

The opening of Brunel's Royal Albert Bridge at Saltash in 1859, linking London with Cornwall, brought new opportunities for trade and tourism to the Penzance area. Travellers bound for St Ives would alight at St Ives Road Station (now St Erth), and complete the journey by horse-drawn omnibus or some other conveyance. A few years later when mining was in decline and fishing less certain, some enterprising citizens of West Penwith who saw the potential of St Ives as a holiday resort, pressed ahead with a branch line, which opened in 1877 amidst enthusiastic celebrations. *Tregenna Castle* became a high class hotel, and hotels and lodging houses of all kinds began to proliferate.

During the course of its construction several skeletons, one 6 ft 4 inches long, were discovered on the Towans, and the possible ruins of the ancient church of St Uny Lelant, along with several promising mineral lodes.

Porthminster Beach, St Ives.

Art and Creativity

An enchanting feature of St Ives is the exceptional clarity of the atmosphere, with its accompanying wonders of colour – glory and reflection; the distant moorlands or the foam flecked sea and rugged rocks, seen through this atmosphere, take on an added glory of form and colour. The most inartistic soul would gaze in wonder at the glorious tints of the flowers and trees, ferns and mosses, ranging from the softest tones to the brightest hues. Guidebook of 1930

A St Ives artist at work.

The influx of visitors brought here by the railway, included artists, who were captivated by the picturesque work-a-day charm of the harbourside, the quaint streets and the vibrant beauty of the landscape. Whistler and Sickert arrived here in 1883, and by the end of that century there was an established colony of artists, using sail lofts and tiny cottages as studios, working at their easels on the quayside, and frequenting the pubs. The *St Ives Society* was founded in 1926. Exhibitions were held in their galleries at Porthmeor, and they gained a worldwide reputation. Although these artists became absorbed into the St Ives scene, there remained a culture gap between this cosmopolitan colony, with their strange goings-on, and the traditional folk of St Ives.

The internationally acclaimed potter Bernard Leach came here in 1920, and Ben Nicholson and the famous sculptress Barbara Hepworth appeared on the scene in the late 1930s. It was Ben Nicholson who recognised the 'untutored genius' of Alfred Wallis, a humble fisherman and rag-and-bone merchant, who was projected to fame but not fortune. He died in Madron Workhouse in 1942. Friction between traditional painters and subsequent arrivals, led to the 'modernists' breaking away in 1949, and setting up the *Penwith Society of Arts*, and various groups and galleries emerged. The modern *Tate Gallery* at Porthmeor continues these traditions of creativity, with a worldwide following.

The writer Virginia Woolf spent happy childhood summers here, staying at Talland House, commanding striking views across the bay. Godrevy Lighthouse on its little island was the inspiration for her novel *To the Lighthouse*.

Tourism

The Cornish Riviera at St Ives station in 1946. This scenic rail route remains one of the finest in the country.

The scenic branch line running along the western side of the Hayle estuary across Lelant Towans through the deep Carrack Gladden cutting to Carbis Bay, over the handsome viaduct which crosses the valley, then winding around the cliffs to St Ives station, remains the ideal introduction to this wonderful environment. Early guidebooks enthused about the quaint old fishing port with its Continental atmosphere, the flower strewn countryside and the exceptionally healthy climate. The run down industrial sites around Carbis Bay were transformed into an amenity area, with trees and pleasant walkways, and bathing machines and 'Pickwick' tents appeared on local beaches. The work of the artists who had taken root here also attracted tourists. By 1900 St Ives had become quite a fashionable watering place, with tasteful terraces and comfortable hotels and boarding houses. The holiday makers took drives around the countryside in horse drawn conveyances and enjoyed the local walks.

By the 1930s visitors could travel by air, as well as road, rail or sea, for there was an airport at St Erth. Some of the smarter hotels, which were AA or RAC appointed, were offering lock-up garages for motorists, and also providing luncheons, afternoon teas and ball suppers. Other diversions included the cinema, concerts, golf, bathing, fishing and boating. Campers and caravanners were free to set up anywhere, with the landowner's permission, as long as they behaved themselves. Social changes after the Second World War brought people from all backgrounds to the resort, which adapted to their needs.

The place known as Carbis Bay was an old fishing cove. The area has seen many changes since the days of a prehistoric settlement, with mining activity, the disruption of creating a viaduct to carry the railway across the Carbis Valley, its rebirth as a recreational area, and the influx of tourists. Houses and flats with desirable sea views now occupy the once industrial terrain. **Carbis Bay**

Lelant, where the mother church of St Ives was situated, was once an important port and prestigious market centre when St Ives was a mere fishing settlement. When the ancient harbour on the tidal estuary at the head of St Ives Bay silted up a certain rivalry arose between Lelant and St Ives. Extensive mining activities in the area were said to have contributed to the decline of Lelant, described in the sixteenth century as being a pretty town with a passage across the strand at low tide. **Lelant**

According to tradition the castle of Theodorick, a rough and ready king of Cornwall who decapitated many of the Irish saints who came here to save souls, lies beneath these sands.

Mid nineteenth century travellers, who took the old route to St Ives over Castle-an-Dinas, enjoyed the spectacular beauty of the flower-strewn slopes above Lelant and Carbis Bay, where fuchsias, hydrangea and myrtle flourished all year round in sheltered cottage gardens. At that time mention was made of a rare and elegant fern growing around the entrance to a damp cave at Carrack Gladden, and rare banded snails in the sandhills.

Nineteenth century tourists hiring horse-drawn conveyances from St Ives enjoyed the exhilarating ride down the western road to Zennor, with the dramatic, craggy landscape on one side, and stunning views of the Atlantic Ocean on the other. Hardy walkers climbed to the summit of *Zennor Hill*, and marvelled at the wonders of Zennor Quoit, a prehistoric chamber tomb with side stones and a massive capstone (now slumped), and the *Logan Stone* (rocking stone), which is a natural phenomenum. This enduring granitic landscape bearing imprints of those who went before us, with their hill forts, villages, cromlechs, barrows and mysterious standing stones, reflects the very essence of prehistoric Cornwall.

Zennor

The Mermaid

The Mermaid, Zennor Church.

The little grey village of Zennor stands on a windswept ledge above the rocky, dramatic coastline in an area of ancient field systems, where the wild and boulder-strewn terrain sweeps down from the high tors. Zennor church, dedicated to St Senner, was given to Tywardreath Priory in 1150, and appropriated to Glasney College, Penryn in 1270. An aisle and tower of three stages were added in the fifteenth century. The most celebrated feature of this ancient church is the carved bench end, now incorporated in a chancel seat, depicting a mermaid with a comb and looking glass in her hands. Legend tells how she stole up to the church from the cove below to listen to the delightful voice of the squire's son Matthew Trewhella as he sang in the choir, and how she eventually lured him away to her watery domain beneath the waves, never to be seen again. The sundial on the church tower, dating from 1737, was the work of Paul Quick, a

relative of Zennor's famous poet Henry Quick. Buried in the churchyard are the two John Daveys, father and son (1770–1844 and 1812–1891), cited by some as being the last to understand the Cornish language, rather than Dolly Pentreath of Paul.

The village enjoys a variety of literary associations, and is the haunt of artists. W.H. Hudson stayed here in 1906 while researching a book about the natural history of the area, and D.H. Lawrence and his German wife Frieda stopped at the *Tinners' Arms* in 1916, whilst house hunting with the aim of creating a small colony of kindred spirits in the area. Having established themselves in a cottage at Higher Tregerthen, they were regarded with suspicion by local folk, who thought they were signalling to German submarines from their cottage window, and they felt obliged to move away. Much of Lawrence's novel *Women in Love* was written here at this time.

Sundial, Zennor Church
1737

Old Mr Barber, who made model boats and crafted dolls known as 'Joannies' from discarded oars.

'Man Friday' Paynter (right), was renowned for his far-fetched yarns about life before the mast in the good old days.

Alfred Wallis, destined to be recognised as a gifted painter of the primitive style standing in a skiff on the right, in the 1890s.

The Old Timers remained part of the maritime scene, and could spend time reminiscing about the days of their youth.